Fox Talbot

An illustrated life of
William Henry Fox Talbot,
'Father of Modern Photography'

1800-1877

John Hannavy

Shire Publications Ltd

2

Contents

ACKNOWLEDGEMENTS

When writing the first edition of this book, I acknowledged the help and guidance given by Mr William Tayler of Lacock for his help in providing information on the history of the village and in providing illustrations; the staff at Lacock for their co-operation and the staff at the Science Museum for their patience in answering all my many queries and requests; the librarians of Manchester, Liverpool and the Technical College in Wigan, together with the National Galleries of Scotland, who all provided invaluable information and support. My greatest thanks, however, went to my late wife, Eileen, for her researches and her tolerance and to John Ward and Bob Lassam for their help in correcting the original typescript. Although it has undergone extensive revision and rewriting for this third edition, the help and advice offered then is still at the heart of the text.

Illustrations are acknowledged as follows: the Science Museum, pages 2, 10, 13 (Crown Copyright), 16-17, 18, 19, 21, 37; the National Galleries of Scotland, page 28; Mr William Tayler of Lacock, page 8; John Hannavy Picture Collection, pages 4, 7, 8 (bottom), 9, 10 (top), 39, 40, 45; Private Collection, pages 14, 46.

The cover photograph by the author shows the lattice window (over the door) in Lacock Abbey, Wiltshire, which was the subject of some of Fox Talbot's earliest photographs.

Printed in Great Britain by CIT Printing Services, Press Buildings, Merlins Bridge, Haverfordwest, Pembrokeshire SA61 1XF.

British Library Cataloguing in Publication Data: Hannavy, John. Fox Talbot: an illustrated life of William Henry Fox Talbot, 'father of modern photography', 1800-1877. - 3rd ed. – (Lifelines; 38) 1. Talbot, William Henry Fox, 1800-1877 2. Photographers – Great Britain – Biography I. Title 770.9'2 ISBN 0 7478 0351 X

Facing page: A portrait of William Henry Fox Talbot, taken by the Edinburgh photographer John Moffat in 1864. Talbot was photographed by several of his contemporaries, including Moffat and Claudet.

Sanderson Miller's west front of Lacock Abbey, Wiltshire, completed in 1754 as part of a major reconstruction of the property in the eighteenth century.

Early genius

The name of William Henry Fox Talbot is synonymous with the development of photography as we know it today. Many of the terms we use in describing photography and the photographic process originate in his early writings and patent specifications on the subject. Today's photography can trace its lineage directly back to his early experiments, and because his home, Lacock Abbey, features in so many of his early images, students of photographic history the world over feel they know the place before they ever visit it.

Fox Talbot's antecedents can be traced back to the mid sixteenth century at Lacock Abbey, Wiltshire, and perhaps further. The abbey itself, originally a nunnery, was founded in April 1232 and housed a convent of Augustinian canonesses. The abbey was a prosperous foundation and the records show that the nuns lived a very comfortable life there. The chapter was expanded through the centuries and the house's riches increased correspondingly, suggesting that the new residents were ladies of some wealth.

However, with the Reformation and the Dissolution of the Monasteries in the sixteenth century, the abbey's religious days came to an end in 1539 when the house was suppressed and the buildings and lands were sold to William Sharrington for the sum of £783. Sharrington was the first of Talbot's forefathers to live at Lacock Abbey and the first of many residents to rebuild, modify or extend the fabric. The abbey to which the young William Henry Fox Talbot eventually became heir was a greatly different building from the abbey of the sixteenth century.

Fox Talbot was born at Melbury in Dorset in 1800, a fact which may seem surprising in view of the length of the family's tenure of the abbey. However, hard times had befallen the family when young Talbot was born. His mother was Lady Elisabeth Fox Strangways and her family's house was at Melbury. Talbot's father, an extravagant officer in the Dragoons, was dead before the child was six months old, leaving enormous debts and little money with which to settle them. Lady Elisabeth's grandfather, the Earl of Ilchester, was unable to help them despite his grand title, and the only way out of their problems was to let Lacock to a wealthy tenant and live wherever they could find shelter. Thus, for several years, the family migrated from the home of one wealthy friend to another. Lady Elisabeth remarried when the boy was four and her second husband was a Captain Feilding, an ambitious naval officer who, despite his affection for his new wife and her son, saw them rarely on account of his naval commitment. So, with an absent husband, the situation was little better than before and young Talbot was still unable to return to his ancestral home and take up residence as the Lord of the Manor which was his right. Luckily stepfather and stepson got on well together and formed a friendship that lasted for the remainder of Captain Feilding's life.

At the age of eight, the boy, known as Henry at home, was sent to boarding school at Rottingdean and almost immediately started to impress his masters by his precise manner and methodical approach to work. For two years prior to starting school he had systematically written down everything he did in a large diary and seems to have had an almost fanatical urge to record every minute of his life and to retain every record. He even instructed his mother and stepfather not to throw away his letters but to store them for the future.

He left Rottingdean to take up a place at Harrow and in 1817 went to Trinity College, Cambridge. He left college at twenty-one, having become, on his birthday, squire of Lacock Abbey. The abbey, however, was still occupied by a tenant with several more years of the lease yet to run, so young Fox Talbot travelled on the continent furthering his studies.

DIVERSITY OF INTERESTS

His interests were many and varied. By 1822 he had been made a member of the Royal Astronomical Society and he made frequent trips back to London for discussions, lectures and meetings. In this way he passed the years until at last, in 1827, he took up residence at Lacock. He modified the house only a little, transforming it into a comfortable and personal place to live. Now, in his own manor, he pursued private studies in physics, chemistry, astronomy and almost every other science that appealed to him. At the age of thirty-one he was admitted to membership of the Royal Society and, amazingly, within a year had been elected to the Fellowship. To have FRS after one's name at the age of thirty-two is indeed rare, but so were Henry's talents. It was, in particular, his writings on the complex subject of mathematics for which he was honoured, having written extensively on the subject for quite some time.

In 1832, in addition to his fellowship of the Royal Society, he added MP to his name, having successfully fought the Chippenham constituency election for the First Reform Parliament. (It is interesting to note that the MP for Rochdale in Lancashire elected at the same time was one John Fenton, father of Roger Fenton who would achieve such fame as a photographer in the 1850s using both the process Talbot was to invent, and also that which Frederick Scott Archer invented to supersede Talbot's calotype.)

In the same year Henry married Constance Mundy of Markeaton in Derbyshire. Because of the pressures of his many interests their honeymoon was delayed until the early autumn of 1833, when the couple visited Italy, where Talbot used his camera obscura to make

Lacock Abbey from the south. The south gallery on the first floor was extensively altered in 1828 by Fox Talbot, to whose design the three oriel windows were constructed. The small central one would be the subject of his first successful camera negative in 1835.

A winding street in Lacock village in Fox Talbot's day (above), with the village carpenter's workshop visible on the right. Joseph Foden, seen here standing outside his workshop in the 1860s, is believed to have made some of the tiny cameras used in Fox Talbot's early experiments in the 1830s.

The same building today (right) is a private dwelling.

Sharrington's Tower (opposite page), built in 1550 on the south-east corner of the abbey, features in many of Talbot's photographs. Beneath the lawns in front of the south face of the building lie the remains of the medieval abbey church.

drawings of Lake Como.

'This led me to reflect on the inimitable beauty of the pictures of nature's painting which the glass lens of the camera obscura throws upon the paper in its focus – fairy pictures, creations of a moment, and destined as rapidly to fade away. It was during these thoughts that the idea occurred to me. . . how charming it would be if it were possible to cause these natural images to imprint themselves durably and fixed upon the paper! And why should that be possible I ask myself?' (Text from Talbot's *The Pencil of Nature*.)

He returned from Italy with some experimental ideas to follow up and his results were sufficiently promising for him to be producing recognisable images by the summer of 1834. His enthusiasm for the process was enormous.

With many demands on his time both from his estates and his varied interests, Henry decided to abandon politics, and when the General Election was announced in 1835 he declined the offer of renomination. The Whigs were left to find a new candidate for the Chippenham constituency.

Much of Talbot's early experimental work was with what we would now know as photograms. He called his process 'Photogenic Drawing' and used it to record images of leaves, etc, and to copy sketches and engravings. However, in 1835 he used this small lattice window (right) above the cloister door at Lacock Abbey as the subject for an early camera negative. The Photogenic Drawing (below) shows the window taken from inside the abbey. In Talbot's own tiny handwriting is the legend: 'Latticed window (with the camera obscura) August 1835. When first made, the squares of glass, about 200 in number, could be counted with the help of a lens.' In Talbot's day, and until relatively recently, the window was surrounded by foliage. The creeper will return over the years.

*Latticed Window
(with the Camera Obscura)
August 1835
When first made, the squares
of glass about 200 in numbers
could be counted, with help
of a lens.*

Research on photography

On his return to the abbey, Talbot devoted himself to developing the ideas which had been germinating in his head while he was in Italy. He was aware of the darkening effect of light upon certain chemicals and began experimenting with silver nitrate brushed on to paper. The sensitivity of these chemicals was very low, however, and his sharp scientific mind suggested a coating first of silver chloride and then of silver nitrate. Although the major proportion of the area showed no marked improvement, Talbot noticed that the edges, where the coating was thinner, showed a marked increase in sensitivity. So, weakening the chloride solution by degrees, he eventually arrived at a composition which gave heightened sensitivity. His process, in its infancy, he called 'Photogenic Drawing' and initially he used it merely to record, by contact, translucent objects such as drawings and leaves. By 1835 he was ready to experiment with photography from nature using small cameras.

Talbot was in a privileged position as squire of Lacock for he owned not only the abbey with its extensive and romantic grounds, but the village as well. All the residents in the village were tenants of the abbey, and many of them were also employees. He is recorded as being a most thoughtful and generous landlord. Rents were low, the squire was generous and was noted by his tenants to be a most friendly and genial man. It is highly likely, therefore, that he would have engaged Joseph Foden, the village carpenter, to assist with the manufacture of small wooden box cameras which he used for his early experiments. As his successes increased, other employees on the Lacock estate were used as subjects for his many experimental images, and for the series of pictures he produced to demonstrate the versatility of his new invention.

THE INVENTION OF PHOTOGRAPHY

Joseph Nicephore Niepce is credited with being the first man in the world to produce a picture in a camera and keep the image visible for long enough to show it off. That was sometime between 1822 and 1826. But he was by no means the only person engaged in photographic

11

experiments at the time, and the British contribution to the development of photography was along much more promising lines than those early Niepce experiments in Chalon-sur-Saône.

Josiah Wedgwood, the potter, had been commissioned to produce a huge dinner service for the Tsar of Russia and each piece of china was to be decorated with a miniature painting of a different English country house. This challenge prompted his son Thomas to follow up some early experiments he had carried out on the problems of producing images by photography. Together with Humphrey Davy (of Safety Lamp fame), Wedgwood all but succeeded. He carried out a series of experiments coating paper, leather and a number of other materials but, although he produced images, he could not arrest the blackening effect of continued exposure to light. Like Talbot, Wedgwood was also working along the lines on which modern photography is based – producing a negative.

In 1839 Louis Jacques Mandé Daguerre, a flamboyant Frenchman, announced his photographic process, only a few weeks before Talbot announced his. The daguerreotype was a direct positive process producing a unique image: it could not be duplicated except by photographing it on to another daguerreotype. It produced a very finely detailed picture, and although very large daguerreotypes were occasionally produced, the majority were in relatively small formats. Most popular sizes were sixth plate and ninth plate – typical miniature painting sizes. In contrast, Talbot's photogenic drawing process, which he made public towards the end of 1839, produced larger pictures of slightly poorer definition. While the daguerreotype was unique, the photogenic drawing process produced a paper negative from which any number of prints could be made. Daguerre used copper plates as the latest in a long line of bases for photography (Niepce had used pewter plates, and Wedgwood both paper and leather). The highly polished plates were chemically coated with silver and sensitised before use. After his early experiments, the absence of any visible image on the plates had caused Daguerre to assume his experiments were failures, but continued work proved the existence of an invisible 'latent' image which could be intensified by further chemical treatment. The idea of 'development' had been born. It is interesting, although a little ironic, that Daguerre's copper plate should prove to be the most successful early process, despite the unique nature of the image. Both Niepce and Wedgwood had carried out early

Talbot's earliest cameras were of very simple design and construction. His mother described some of them as 'Henry's little mousetraps' by virtue of their apparent resemblance to Victorian traps designed to trap rather than kill mice!

experiments using paper as a base, producing a negative image (or as they both commented, an image in which the lights and shades were reversed) but had abandoned them. Wedgwood abandoned his experiments because he could not stop the image blackening in light. Had he done a little reading, he would have found that some years earlier Herschel had identified common salt as being a chemical which would do just that. Daguerre also used common salt in his early experiments, later turning to sodium thiosulphate, the fixer still widely used today. Daguerre's process became widely popular and many thousands of photographic portrait studios opened up throughout the world using his process. The experiments abandoned by both Niepce and Daguerre in favour of direct positive processes would later prove to have been the correct path when Talbot's experiments bore fruit.

There is little doubt that the photogenic drawing process was of limited use, although Talbot made fine studies both by contact (of leaves, lace and so on) and using a camera. The well-known view of the lattice window at Lacock is a photogenic drawing, but the length of exposure required was too long. But continued work by Talbot soon reduced that time. Late in 1840 he too found that after a short exposure there was a latent image which could be 'developed' and 'fixed'. He called this new process the 'calotype' or 'Talbotype'. Talbot used

13

Melrose Abbey in the Scottish borders (above) was one of the subjects Talbot photographed for 'Sun Pictures in Scotland', published in 1845 and celebrating the life and writings of Sir Walter Scott. About one hundred and twenty copies of the book were produced, each with twenty-three calotypes – a total of over two thousand seven hundred hand-made prints.

The announcement of 'Sun Pictures in Scotland' (right) heralded the publication of Talbot's first complete book project. 'The Pencil of Nature', although announced in 1844, was published intermittently as a partwork between 1844 and 1846.

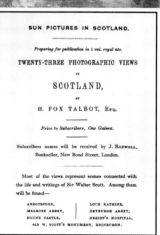

SUN PICTURES IN SCOTLAND.

Preparing for publication in 1 vol. royal 4to.

TWENTY-THREE PHOTOGRAPHIC VIEWS

IN

SCOTLAND,

BY

H. FOX TALBOT, Esq.

Price to Subscribers, One Guinea.

Subscribers names will be received by J. RODWELL, Bookseller, New Bond Street, London.

Most of the views represent scenes connected with the life and writings of Sir Walter Scott. Among them will be found—

ABBOTSFORD,	LOCH KATRINE,
MELROSE ABBEY,	DRYBURGH ABBEY,
DOUNE CASTLE,	HERIOT'S HOSPITAL,
SIR W. SCOTT'S MONUMENT, EDINBURGH.	

14

sensitised paper as his base and produced, in the camera, a negative image. This image was later placed in a printing frame with a new sheet of sensitised paper behind it and, after exposure, a print was produced by contact. However, no development was used for the print. Talbot merely gave a long exposure until an image appeared on the paper – by the action of light alone – as he had with his earlier 'photogenic drawings'. The image was then fixed in common salt. Talbot therefore has a solid claim to be referred to as the 'father of modern photography', just as the daguerreotype is often referred to as photography's 'false start'. As to a description of Talbot's process, who better than Talbot himself to describe it. These following lines are taken from the Patent Specification for the Calotype Process, Patent No. 8842, 1841, filed by Talbot himself and reproduced by permission of the Patents Office.

PHOTOGRAPHIC PICTURES AD 1841 NO. 8842

To all to whom these presents shall come, I William Henry Fox Talbot of Lacock Abbey in the county of Wilts, Esquire, send greetings. Whereas Her present most Excellent Majesty Queen Victoria, by Her Letters Patent under the Great Seal of Great Britain, bearing date at Westminster the Eighth day of February in the fourth year of her reign, did, for herself, her heirs and successors, give and grant unto me, the said William Henry Fox Talbot, Her Especial Licence, full power, sole privilege and authority, that I, the said William Henry Fox Talbot, my executors, administrators and assigns, or such others as I, the said William Henry Fox Talbot, my executors, administrators or assigns, should at any time agree with, and no others, from time to time and at all times during the term of years expressed therein, should and lawfully might make, use, exercise and vend, within England, Wales and the Town of Berwick-upon-Tweed, my invention of *'Improvements in Obtaining Pictures or Representations of Objects'.*

The first part of my invention is a method of making paper extremely sensitive to the rays of light. For this purpose I select the best writing paper having a smooth surface and a close even texture.

First Part of the Preparation of the Paper: I dissolve one hundred grains of crystallised nitrate of silver in six ounces of distilled water. I wash one side of the paper with this solution with a soft camel hair brush, and place a mark on that side by which to know it again. I dry

Talbot's printing establishment at Reading was photographed in two sections to form what is probably photography's first 'panoramic' picture. A photographer, believed to be Talbot himself, is seen in the centre of the photograph, setting up a camera for portraiture. To his left, another photographer is copying an engraving while, to the right, the laborious and time-consuming task of daylight printing is underway.

the paper cautiously at a distant fire or else I leave it to dry spontaneously in a dark place. Next, I dip the paper in a solution of iodide of potassium, containing five hundred grains of that salt dissolved in one pint of water. I leave the paper a minute or two in this solution. I then take it out and dip it in water, I then dry it lightly with blotting paper and finish drying it at a fire; or else I leave it to dry spontaneously; all this process is best done in the evening by candlelight. The paper thus far prepared may be called, for distinction, 'iodised paper'. This iodised paper is scarcely sensitive to light but, nevertheless, it should be kept in a portfolio or some dark place until wanted for use; it does not spoil by keeping any length of time provided it is kept in a portfolio, and not exposed to the light.

Second Part of the Preparation of the Paper: This second part is

best deferred until the paper is wanted for use; when that time is arrived, I take a sheet of the iodised paper, and wash it with a liquid prepared in the following manner:– Dissolve one hundred grains of crystallised nitrate of silver in two ounces of distilled water; to this solution add one-sixth of its volume of strong acetic acid; let this mixture be called A. Dissolve crystallised gallic acid in distilled water as much as it will dissolve (which is a very small quantity); let this solution be called B. When you wish to prepare a piece of paper for use mix together the two liquids A and B in equal volumes. This mixture I shall call by the name of gallo-nitrate of silver. Let no more be mixed than is intended to be used at one time, because the mixture will not keep good for a long period. Then take a sheet of iodised paper and wash it over with this gallo-nitrate of silver with a soft camel hair brush, taking care to wash it on the side which has been previously marked. This operation should be performed by candlelight. Let the paper rest half a minute, and then dip it into water, then dry it lightly with blotting paper, and lastly, dry it cautiously at a fire, holding it a

17

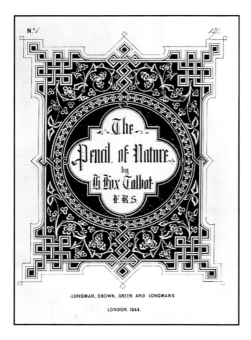

39, *Paternoster Row, London,*
June, 1844.

JUST PUBLISHED,

PART I.

OF

THE PENCIL OF NATURE,

BY

H. FOX TALBOT, ESQ.

THE new art of PHOTOGRAPHY was announced to the world almost simultaneously in France and England, at the commencement of the year 1839, by M. Daguerre and by the author of the present work. The processes employed were at first kept secret, but when they became known they were found to be exceedingly different. The French method, which has received the name of the Daguerreotype, is executed upon plates of polished silver, while paper is employed in the English process. The Daguerreotype is now well known to the public, having been extensively used for taking portraits from the life, while the English art (called PHOTOGENIC DRAWING, or the CALOTYPE) has been hitherto chiefly circulated in private societies, and is consequently less generally known.

It has been thought, therefore, that a collection of genuine specimens of the art, in most of its branches, cannot fail to be interesting to a large class of persons who have hitherto had no opportunity of seeing any well-executed specimens. It must

Talbot was quick to realise the importance of his invention to the world of publishing. Hitherto, books had been illustrated with line drawings and engravings. Now, with photography, high-quality illustration was possible – at a price. When the first part of 'The Pencil of Nature' was published in 1844 (above left), it was widely purchased and highly acclaimed. Although, as with all partworks, demand reduced as publication continued, Talbot's epic work changed the face of publishing forever. Like 'Sun Pictures in Scotland', published in the following year, every illustration had to be pasted on to the pages of the book by hand. This hugely labour-intensive operation commanded a high cover price.

(Facing page) In his caption to 'The Ladder', one of the plates in 'The Pencil of Nature', Talbot revealed the true purpose of his publication – it was designed to stimulate public interest in photography in general, and the calotype in particular. His comments, directed at an audience quite ignorant of photography's capabilities, clearly draw attention to what he saw as photography's advantage over painting – the sheer speed at which portraits could be made. He wrote: 'When the sun shines, small portraits can be obtained by my process in one or two seconds, but large portraits require a somewhat longer time. When the weather is dark and cloudy, a corresponding allowance is necessary and a greater demand is made upon the patience of the sitter. Groups of figures require no longer time to obtain than single figures would require, since the camera depicts them all at once, however numerous they

may be, but at present we cannot well succeed in this branch of art without some previous concern and arrangement. But when a group of persons has been artistically arranged, and trained by a little practice to maintain absolute immobility for a few seconds of time, very delightful pictures are easily obtained'. The location for this and many other plates in the book was his Lacock estate. This view can still be seen in the stable block today.

19

considerable distance therefrom. When dry the paper is fit for use, but it is advisable to use it within a few hours after its preparation. (Note, that if it is used immediately the last drying may be dispensed with, and the paper may be used moist.)

Use of the Paper: The paper thus prepared, and which I name 'calotype paper', is placed in a camera obscura, so as to receive the image formed in the focus of the lens; of course the paper must be screened or defended from the light during the time it is being put in the camera. When the camera is properly pointed at the object, the screen is withdrawn, or a pair of internal folding doors are opened, so as to expose the paper for the reception of the image. If the object is very bright, or the time employed is sufficiently long, a sensible image is perceived upon the paper when it is withdrawn from the camera. But when the time is short, or the objects dim, no image whatsoever is visible on the paper, which appears entirely blank. Nevertheless it is impressed with an invisible image; and I have discovered the means of causing this image to become visible. This is performed as follows:– I take some gallo-nitrate of silver, prepared in the manner before directed, and with this liquid I wash the paper all over with a soft camel hair brush. I then hold it before a gentle fire, and in short time (varying from a few seconds to a minute or two) the image begins to appear on the paper. Those parts of the paper upon which light has acted most strongly become brown or black, while those parts on which light has not acted remain white. The image continues to strengthen and grow more visible during some time. When it appears strong enough, the operation should be terminated and the picture fixed.

The Fixing Process: In order to fix the picture thus obtained, I first dip it into water. I then partly dry it with blotting paper and then wash it with a solution of bromide of potassium, containing one hundred grains of that salt dissolved in eight or ten ounces of water. The picture is then washed with water and then finally dried. Instead of bromide of potassium, a strong solution of common salt may be used but it is less advisable. The picture thus obtained will have its lights and shades reversed with respects to the natural objects; videlicet, the lights of the objects are represented by shades and vice versa. But it is easy from this picture to obtain another, which shall be conformable with nature videlicet in which the lights will be represented by lights and the shades by shades....

The Hungerford suspension bridge in London (above), built by Isambard Kingdom Brunel, was photographed by Talbot almost immediately after its completion in 1845.

Calotype printing was a very slow procedure, dependent on lengthy exposure to daylight. Mrs John Dillwyn Llewellyn (left), a first cousin to Fox Talbot, watches a print exposing in the sunlight at Lacock.

Thus Talbot outlined the process he patented. It is interesting to note that through the carelessness of the officials who allowed him to file this specification, or for some other unknown reason, he was thereby allowed to patent 'iodised paper', which had been available commercially for two years previously. Nor was the use of gallic acid original, but its use to develop a latent image was. The Reverend J. B. Reade had experimented with it in 1839, as had Talbot, and it is perhaps possible that Reade's experiments were first. However, Reade himself acknowledged that in the idea of development of the latent image Talbot was working with ideas of which he, Reade, had not even dreamed.

It has often been argued that the wide-ranging nature of the matters covered by Talbot's patent made it highly restrictive. By his patent of 1843, besides other things, he managed to claim the discovery of the use of hyposulphites of soda for fixing, when Herschel had shown that this could be done four years previously. Talbot also mentioned in that patent the smearing of wax into the negative paper in order to render it more transparent for printing, a fact he was later to use in attempts to control the use of Gustave le Gray's Waxed Paper Process in England (le Gray's process differed basically from Talbot's in that le Gray waxed the paper before taking the negative and not after it had been processed). One apparently original innovation in Talbot's 1843 process was the use of a warm plate at the back of the camera to increase the speed of the calotype paper, thereby further reducing the exposure times necessary.

There is little doubt that Talbot had a great deal to which he could lay claim, but in order to protect his inventions his patents seem to be much more embracing than they needed to be. There does appear to be, in his and many other nineteenth-century patents, evidence of a belief that the inventor could patent abstract ideas and patent an end-product with little reference to the means of producing that product. In that respect, Talbot's patents are no more or less restrictive than many others which date from the same period.

Indeed, as a patent's sole purpose was to protect the rights of the inventor to profit from his invention, Talbot's vigorous protection of his rights can be understood. However, his basic misconception of the protection offered by his patents was to cause a great deal of legal wrangling in the years to follow.

Engines

Talbot's interests embraced a wide range of subjects. We have already touched upon his enthusiasm for every subject he tackled. His mastery of Greek and Hebrew and his command of mathematics were but a few of his talents. Other sides of the man were revealed in the numerous patent specifications he filed throughout the 1840s and 1850s.

In 1840 'Obtaining Motive Power' Patent No. 8650 covered several means of obtaining power from ingeniously designed engines. One such engine, part electric motor and part internal combustion engine, sought to use an electric current first to decompose water by electrolysis and second to explode the resultant gases, thereby transmitting power to a piston. The circuit breaker was a cleverly designed flywheel, part metal and part wood, which was in turn driven by the piston to continue the sequence of events. The design was simple: dilute sulphuric acid in the bottom of a sealed chamber with the electrodes submerged in the liquid. Two wires on a separate circuit were suspended above the liquid in the chamber to explode the gases as soon as a current passed across them. The top of the chamber was a cylinder in which a piston could move freely up and down attached to a flywheel.

A second engine described in the same patent was a simple magnetic electric motor (of rather original design – as were all Talbot's inventions). A third and even more unusual motor gained its power from the rapid heating and cooling of a liquid in a sealed tube causing thrust to a piston by virtue of the increase and decrease of pressure.

In 1841 Talbot was patenting methods of plating metals with other rare metals by what appears to be a form of chemical substitution dependent on the action of weak acids. This system is not unlike the effect witnessed by every amateur photographer when he drops a coin into heavily used fixer: the silver is deposited on the coin by displacement of the surface metal. A more refined answer to the same problem was patented by him in the following year.

His 'Obtaining and Applying Motive Power' patent in 1845 was a reversion to the 1840 ideas of heating and cooling liquids, and a full understanding of the ideas expressed in the long and complicated document requires considerable technical knowledge.

By far the most interesting of Talbot's patents appeared in 1846.

23

With the same title, 'Obtaining and Applying Motive Power', Talbot outlined a most ingenious internal combustion engine which can only be described as a variation on a machine-gun. Into a sealed cylinder, with a freely moving piston at the top attached to a flywheel, Talbot suggests that a belt containing pellets of gun-cotton at regular intervals be inserted through an airtight hole. The end of the belt would be attached to the flywheel and the wheel would be of such a size that one revolution will move the belt sufficiently to draw one pellet out of the cylinder and replace it with another. Over the top of the pellet in the cylinder would be two electric wires through which a current could be passed, according to the position of electric contacts on the flywheel. Such a current would be sufficiently large to cause a spark. So, with one pellet in the cylinder, the circuit would be completed. The spark would explode the gun-cotton, which would then move the piston up, thereby turning the flywheel. The wheel would draw the next pellet into position and the process would be repeated. The only limitation on the length of the time for which the motor could be kept running would be the length of the belt of pellets.

Other patented ideas included an engine driven by the rapid expansion characteristics of frozen carbonic acid 'snow' when blown over a heated wire. That same (1845) patent also explored a number of ideas based on the power potential of liquids with large expansion potential when heated.

It also contained outlines of wind and water turbine engines, and a novel approach to reducing friction in an atmospheric railway. Atmospheric railways were much in the news in Talbot's day, especially the 1840s, with many inventors thoroughly convinced that the atmospheric railway was the transport system of the future. At the time this patent specification was being filed, a 2 mile (3.2 km) stretch of atmospheric railway was already operating in Ireland between Kingstown and Dalkey, and experimental work was being carried out on the South Devon Railway. Success eluded all those who sought to bring about that revolution.

However Patent No.10539 AD1845 is perhaps the most wide-ranging of all Talbot's patents, containing no less than eight different ideas for power generation. None of the ideas contained within its pages ever went into production.

Patents and problems

By 1847, the use of Talbot's process, although quite widespread, was far less than it might have been had patents not been so rigorously enforced. Both the daguerreotype and the calotype were covered by very detailed patents, and every photographer who wished to use either process required a licence – issued by Richard Beard in the case of the daguerreotype, and Talbot for the calotype. In those days before mass production, when every photographer prepared his own materials at home, fees from licences were an inventor's only way of seeking a return on his investment and discovery.

The popularity of the daguerreotype, producing a small and lavishly

'Taking a Calotype' demonstrates two important differences between the calotype and its rival, the daguerreotype. Firstly, by the size of the camera, the larger size of the calotype is evident, but secondly, the coarse image quality was considered to be the major drawback of the calotype.

packaged portrait akin to a miniature painting, made the high fees required by the patent holder a worthwhile investment. The commercial applications of the calotype were fewer and less profitable, so licences promised less certain returns. A number of leading photographers, both amateur and professional, produced some remarkable images with the process, however, and a small group of them, led by Peter Fry, joined together in 1847 to form a Photographic Club, sometimes nowadays referred to as the Calotype Club. The original members of this august body were Peter Fry (the founder), Robert Hunt (Keeper at the Museum of Geology), Frederick Scott Archer (who would later invent the wet plate process which rendered the calotype obsolete), Dr Hugh Diamond, Peter le Neve Foster (barrister and Secretary of the Society of Arts), Sir William Newton, Hugh Owen, Joseph Cundall, Edward Kater, Charles Vignoles (civil engineer) and Frederick Berger. These men met in each other's houses to discuss their current work and to talk about possible extensions and improvements to the process.

Talbot by this time had set up a printing establishment at Reading, where he and his assistant took and printed a vast number of their photographs. In fact his valet and assistant reached such proficiency that, for a time, he was official photographer to Queen Victoria.

However, after initial euphoria, many workers quickly became critical of the coarse grain of the calotype and sought to improve it – or even replace it. One of that number, Frederick Scott Archer, experimented with possible substitutes for the paper base. By the end of the decade the Frenchman Gustave le Gray had produced his highly sophisticated Waxed Paper Process, but Talbot had successfully claimed that it was amply catered for in his patent by the phrase: 'I claim...secondly the making of visible photographic images upon paper and the strengthening of such images when already faintly or imperfectly visible by washing them with liquids....' With that all-embracing statement, Talbot, in his patents, sought to exercise control over all processes involving development of photographic paper. Until a test case proved otherwise, his patents, on first inspection, therefore seemed to cover all processes up to the invention of collodion on glass.

Archer had originally tried using collodion as a base (this is a derivative of gun-cotton which was used extensively in the sealing of wounds on hospitalised patients) but later found that the best answer was to suspend the sensitive emulsion in collodion and spread the mixture on

'The Open Door', one of the plates from 'The Pencil of Nature', is one of Talbot's creative masterpieces. There are a number of variants of the image, in which Talbot experiments with tonal qualities, contrast and the depth of shadows, but the basic geometry of the image is masterful.

to glass. Thus the glass plate, popular for a time in the 1840s with Niepce de St Victor's albumen on glass process, proved to be the ideal base for photography: no texture, rigid, reasonably strong and, after slight modification of the original process, capable of recording very fine details with an emulsion speed higher than anything hitherto available.

It appeared to the many practising photographers that Talbot's control over all aspects of photography was ended. However, Talbot was quite adamant about the process – his patents, he said, still held.

By this time, Roger Fenton and a group of other photographers were exploring the idea of forming a London Photographic Society and these discussions eventually led to an inaugural meeting early in 1853. The chair was taken by Sir Charles Eastlake, President of the Royal Academy.

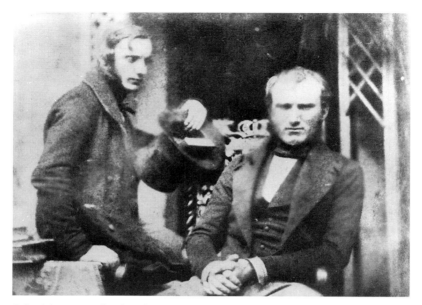

John Adamson and Robert Adamson, photographed by D. O. Hill. Talbot's patents did not cover Scotland, and yet it was in Scotland that the process found its finest exponents. Dr John Adamson of St Andrews University, having himself learned the calotype from Sir David Brewster, in turn taught his son Robert. In collaboration with David Octavius Hill, Robert Adamson produced some of the finest calotypes ever taken, depicting life in Edinburgh and its environs. Included in their output were portraits of the leading figures of early Victorian Edinburgh. Unfortunately, Robert Adamson died in 1848, bringing the partnership to an end.

In recognition of his pivotal position in the evolution of photography, the chair had originally been offered to Fox Talbot but he had declined. The formation of the society, however, had been possible only as a result of a great deal of hard work and negotiation.

At the inaugural meeting, Roger Fenton read a report of the proceedings of the provisional committee during the negotiations which had been carried out: 'The want of a centre of union is not now felt for the first time amongst photographers. Attempts were made at an early period in the history of the art to establish some kind of co-operation among those who were devoting their attention to this study. At that time, however, the number of persons so engaged was so limited, that no organisation of an extensive character was possible. A club, however, was formed and meetings were periodically held at the houses of members of it, and it is beyond a doubt that the progress of the art was thereby much advanced, and many of the difficulties which we should otherwise have now to encounter were cleared out of the way. Some of the gentlemen forming part of that club have rendered the most effective assistance in the construction of what we may now call a Permanent Photographic Society. In the winter of 1851-2, it appeared as if the time were come for more vigorous exertions. The impulse given by the Great Exhibition had so increased the number of photographers, and the art itself had, by the competition and the comparison which that exhibition induced, been so improved, that it was evident it was about to enter into a new phase of its history. The formation of a Society in Paris, showing the views of our neighbours as to the necessity of methodical co-operation, was an additional confirmation of the opinions entertained as to the necessity of an English Photographic Society. With these views, a committee was formed, and met for the first time at the office of the *Art Journal*. At the very threshold of their undertaking, they were met by a difficulty arising from the existence of a patent taken out by Mr Talbot, the inventor of the art. To do away with this difficulty, a meeting was arranged between Mr Talbot and the committee, and the subject was thoroughly discussed, with an earnest desire on the part of the committee and the patentee to arrive at a satisfactory arrangement. Unfortunately, an independent society was found incompatible with the existence of the patent, and the committee was therefore adjourned *sine die*. In the course of the proceedings, however, there was shown a strong feeling in the public mind as to the desirableness of a society, and the number of persons willing to join was so considerable that the committee foresaw that their present failure could only be of a temporary kind. It was now obvious that at this time the existence of the patent was the great obstacle, not only to the formation of the society but to the improvement of the art itself. Few were willing to expend much time and labour upon the art, upon the study of which they were told they had no right to enter without permission. As it was known that Mr Talbot's object in taking out the patent had been principally to establish definitely his claim to the invention, it was resolved to represent all these circumstances to him. Sir C. Eastlake and Lord Rosse, as the official representatives of art and science in this country, kindly undertook to be the exponents of the general feeling; and on receipt of a letter from them, Mr Talbot abandoned the patent so far as was possible consistently with existing engagements. No difficulty now remained, and accordingly at the commencement of the present season the committee was called together again, and a society constituted, which we are now met to formally inaugurate.'

Thus Fenton briefly recalled the negotiations with Talbot which had been so central to the advance of photography in England. And it was only England, Wales and Berwick-upon-Tweed. Talbot's patents, like Beard's daguerreotype patents, excluded Scotland. Presumably the additional cost of separate registration under Scots law was not considered financially sound.

Thus, north of the border, experimentation with the calotype, and indeed some modification of it, went on apace, with Talbot's knowledge, blessing and participation.

South of the border, one outcome of these negotiations was an agreement that, once an undertaking had been given not to use the process for profit – and to buy the iodised paper from Henneman – amateurs would be excluded from his licence requirements. However, despite the gesture made by Fox Talbot in releasing amateurs and artists from his patents, he still insisted that those involved in professional portraiture should be licensed by him. This was to cover establishments which were already in operation licensed by Talbot and providing him with a healthy income.

By the early 1850s, however, most photographers were using either Gustave le Gray's Waxed Paper Process or the wet plate collodion method. Fenton himself, who had been so central to the decision by Talbot, was himself currently using waxed paper and by 1855, when taking his historic series of the Crimean War, had progressed on to glass plates.

Scott Archer had openly published details of the wet plate process (collodion) in the *Chemist* magazine in 1851 and, not surprisingly, a number of photographers turned to the new method, which had been presented to the nation's photographers without condition or restriction. Talbot, still certain that he had patented the idea rather than a specific process, initiated a number of actions for infringements of his patents. Many of the photographers he charged with the 'offence' did not risk challenging his solicitor's charges but merely paid up and applied for a licence. One gentleman, however, Silvester Laroche, decided to stand

To Mr. N. HENNEMAN,

Sun Picture Rooms,

122, Regent Street, London.

Sir,

Understanding that the Patentee of the Photographic process, known as the Talbotype or Calotype, has no objection to that process being used by Amateurs, who pledge themselves to use it BONA FIDE, FOR THE PURPOSE OF AMUSEMENT ONLY; and that they will purchase from your Establishment the Iodised Paper belonging to the said Patent Invention, which they may require and also that they will not make any such use of the Art as to interfere injuriously with your Establishment, but will immediately discontinue any such use of it, on your requesting them to do so. Now, I being desirous of practising the aforesaid Patent Invention as an Amateur only, and without any view to profit, either directly or indirectly, am willing to give you the pledge and assurance above mentioned.

Witness my hand, at   this   day of   in the year 184

Witness to Signature

The agreement which Talbot drew up for amateurs to sign, freeing them from having to pay for a calotype licence.

his ground and there followed a memorable lawsuit.

TALBOT V. LAROCHE 1854

The calotype patents were due for renewal in 1854, by which time collodion was winning favour throughout Britain. The announcement by Talbot of his intention to renew his patents and to continue to enforce them brought the members of the Photographic Society together for an emergency meeting. At the meeting, Silvester Laroche, who had received a writ from Talbot's solicitors, made it clear that he intended to fight and called on his fellow photographers for contributions to his fighting fund. The effect of this summons was striking. As long as Talbot had not actively pursued those who contravened his patents, a number of interested parties had stayed out of the limelight. Now, however, to

31

Lacock Abbey seen across the river Avon. This early calotype was used as one of the plates for the book 'The Pencil of Nature'.

Laroche's aid came the Reverend J. B. Reade, whose researches in the 1830s had been usually parallel to and occasionally a little ahead of Talbot's. With Reade by his side, in effect Laroche declared war on Talbot. What had started as a simple case of Laroche defending his rights to use the wet plate process had now become an attempt to determine whether or not Talbot was the inventor of the calotype – a fact which should never have been in dispute. How many inventors of great renown could honestly claim that every detail of their invention was original, for obviously the knowledge of others forms the basis upon which they built? Talbot admitted during the case that Reade's first experiments had been communicated to him in the early days. Laroche's counsel was clearly aiming not only to defend his client's action but to discredit Talbot. The case lasted three days, during which argument often became heated and, when the jury eventually returned with its verdict, neither

This very late calotype view of Lacock's west front was taken by Talbot himself in 1861. It is remarkably coarse for the period as, by this time, Talbot was producing very finely detailed images.

man really won nor lost. Laroche was found not guilty of infringing Talbot's patents but Talbot was determined, in law, to be the true inventor of the calotype process. For Talbot it was a partial victory. His title as inventor was reinforced but his claim over all the other processes in use was gone forever. He decided not to renew his patents, an occasion which almost coincided with the relaxation of Daguerre's patents, and for the first time every photographic process was free of restriction. However, not everybody profited as a result. Both Talbot and Daguerre had profited from their inventions, Daguerre much more than Talbot, but Scott Archer, whose free gift of the wet plate process had made photography so widely accessible, died penniless.

Talbot continued to use his own process and for most of his time turned his attention to inventions in allied fields and also to his many other interests.

Fox Talbot's calotype of York Minster shows early evidence of the camera's tendency to cause converging verticals when tilted upwards. The 'tilt' control can be seen on the left-hand camera illustrated on page 13.

Photoglyphic Engraving

Almost from the first moments of photography, its application to engraving and multiple photo-mechanical printing was seen as a vital and integral part of the process's development. Niepce's earliest experiments were involved with the production of printing plates via photography.

Photography gave hitherto undreamed-of quality for illustrations but its cost made it impractical for book illustration, despite Talbot's success with *The Pencil of Nature* and *Sun Pictures in Scotland*. So Talbot turned his attention to the challenge of evolving an engraving process which used photographic originals and which would retain the mid-tone, that unique characteristic of the photograph.

When the Great Exhibition was held in 1851, Talbot and Henneman had been commissioned to photograph all the exhibits and original salt prints were used in the bound volumes of the judge's reports. The use of actual prints was possible because only a few copies of the reports were being prepared. For the mass market, the published accounts of the exhibition used engravings based on daguerreotypes by J. E. Mayall. By using daguerreotypes as no more than reference, the engraver was free to add people to his pictures, thus giving them an immediacy which both Mayall's and Talbot's pictures lacked. Within a year of the exhibition, Talbot had filed a provisional specification for a patent process of photo-engraving.

That patent, No. 565 for 1852 and filed on 29th October, was the culmination of at least a year's research and showed the extent of Talbot's experimentation. Judging by examples of his work from this period, he had achieved some limited success.

The process used an engraver's steel plate, made light-sensitive with a coating of bichromated gelatin 'such as when cold coagulates into firm jelly'. In its earliest form, the process involved the simple contact exposure of a leaf or some other simple natural form. After an exposure of from two to five minutes in strong sunshine, an image of the leaf was produced on to the plate, the bichromated gelatin having been hardened and turned brown by exposure, with the unexposed areas remaining yellow beneath the subject.

The unhardened area was then washed off and the plate plunged

35

into an alcohol bath to remove the water. After drying, the plate was etched in the normal way. The etching complete, the remaining gelatin was removed and the plate cleaned in a salt solution before being dried. It could then be inked and used to print a limited number of impressions. Talbot specified waxing of the etched plate to counter the effects of rusting from the atmosphere.

Talbot also specified several modifications to the process, each of which slightly improved the image quality possible. The most important of these involved the 'laying down' of a regular pattern or screen on to the plate, using either muslin or crepe, before the contact exposure to the actual subject was made, improving the mid-tones. Thus the areas which had in the first version remained unexposed owing to their position beneath the subject were given a short pre-exposure, reducing the black to a dark grey. With these variations he produced softer images.

He additionally hinted at the possibility of using a resin ground and commented that the alcohol wash to speed drying would have to be eliminated if this variant was used, for the alcohol would dissolve the resin. As the resin was laid on to the plate before the bichromated gelatin, that would have effectively removed the entire image! This variation was similar to the aquatint process, already known to contemporary engravers.

Typical of the imprecise wording of Victorian patents, he also mentioned that the use of the word 'gelatin' did not mean that he excluded all other vehicles for the potassium bichromate coating. He mentioned other substances such as albumen, isinglass or gum arabic 'and other analogous substances in various proportions'. That single sentence at the end of the specification was to be the cause of a lot of trouble in years to come.

Six years later, his 1858 patent described the process he called 'Photoglyphic Engraving': 'I then take a warm slab of gutta-percha and press it on to the metal plate in a press; it will then take the impression of the design or picture on the metal plate; I then electrotype the gutta-percha having first made its surface conductive of electricity, and thus I obtain an electrotyped etching; and to the process herein described I have given the name of photo-glyphic engraving.'

Thus in the original specification, albeit provisional, Talbot clearly intended that 'Photoglyphic Engraving' should be a term restricted to his electrolytic process. However, by the time the full specification

This example of an etching made using a 'coarse resin ground' dates from 1854. Although showing some mid-tones, this early example is well short of the quality Talbot was seeking.

was published, he was using the term 'Photoglyphic Engraving' to describe all the process variants contained in that 1858 patent.

The clearest difference between the 1852 and 1858 patents was in the application of the 'ground'. By 1858 he had discovered that the use of a fine gum ground after exposure – and on top of the gelatin – gave a much better basis for printing.

The gum or resin was dusted on to the exposed gelatin layer and then heated from below with a strong flame until it melted. The plate was then cooled and etched as before. The main differences were, first, that he no longer considered it necessary to wash off the unhardened bichromate and gelatin before etching; and, most important, that he laid the ground on after the gelatin, instead of before. These two variations apparently greatly increased his success rate, and 1858 examples of the process clearly show mid-tones, even if they are not yet as subtle as he wished.

By the early 1860s, Talbot appears to have changed direction somewhat and was experimenting with reticulated resin grounds. In doing this he was virtually repeating work carried out a few years earlier by Paul Pretsch.

That in itself is an interesting point, for at one time he had threatened Pretsch with legal action for infringements of his (Talbot's) patents. Yet by looking closely at Pretsch's 1854 patent, and comparing it with the provisional specification for Talbot's 1858 Photoglyphic Engraving process (the electrotype version), it appears that Talbot had described a process which Pretsch could very reasonably have assumed was covered by his own patents.

In Patent No. 2373 of 1854 Paul Pretsch was working from a collodion-based image (rather than gelatin-dusted) and the relief image this produced was dusted with graphite and then built up into a thin relief metal image by electrolysis.

In the best Victorian patent tradition, Pretsch did not limit himself to collodion but mentioned gelatin, isinglass and, for good measure, added the sentence 'As my invention is capable of being variously modified, I do not restrict myself to the precise processes described, nor to any particular chemical ingredients or photographic or galvanic apparatus . . .'

While Talbot might have had grounds for suing Pretsch for limited infringements of his 1852 patent, Pretsch might well have sued Talbot in 1858 as the latter's 1858 patent apparently covered processes and ideas already clearly laid out by Pretsch four years earlier.

It is curious that, although Pretsch's patent was issued in 1854 and by 1855 he had gone into production through his Photo-Galvanographic Company and the good offices of his chief photographer Roger Fenton, Talbot did not immediately challenge him. Indeed *Photographic Art Treasures*, Pretsch's first commercial venture, had come and gone – as had the company itself – before he first felt Talbot's wrath. The first threatened action – in 1857 – was apparently dropped, but Pretsch's second encounter with Talbot came in 1859 when the editor of the *Manchester Photographic Journal* promised his readers that he would publish a plate produced by the Pretsch process, which had only recently ceased to need a great deal of help from the retoucher's pen. Talbot issued a summons and the magazine, unsure of its position, backed down and declined to publish.

Pretsch, now working for de la Rue, had announced a lithographic variation on his photo-galvanographic process. Talbot had mentioned the possibility of using his own process on litho stone in his 1852 patent and felt that was justification enough for legal action.

It might be argued that Pretsch's patent of 1854 infringed Talbot's 1852 specification – at least by implication, if not backed by clear proof of experimental success. The wording of both men's patents was imprecise in the extreme and would never be allowed today. The ambiguous nature of several of Talbot's patents often clouds the truly impressive work he undertook.

Either man could be held to have borrowed ideas from the other –

The fifteenth-century cloisters of the Augustinian nunnery (top) and the sixteenth-century stables built by William Sharrington were both frequent subjects for Talbot's camera.

or neither. The basis of both processes was bichromated gelatin, collodion or a variety of other carriers, and there were many researchers pursuing similar ideas. The basic idea was also used in the collotype, Autotype and Woodburytype processes in the following decade. Pretsch's process

Lacock village is now owned and managed by the National Trust, which seeks to ensure that its eighteenth-century character is not marred by inappropriate developments. Henry Fox Talbot would find it little changed from his day.

died out within a very few years while the essence of Talbot's work was consolidated by Karl Klic in his grain photogravure process of the late 1870s.

Last years

The threatened lawsuit against Pretsch and his publishers was the closing chapter of Talbot's involvement with the photographic world. Although he continued to take photographs himself, he contributed nothing further to the development of the art.

THE RECLUSE

Back in 1851 his knowledge of Hebrew and Greek had led to his involvement in the transcription and translation of cuneiform inscriptions from 1300 BC in Assyria and it was with projects of this nature that he now concerned himself. He offered his knowledge and skills during the archaeological excavations at Nineveh, once more on cuneiform inscriptions, and in his spare time continued his studies and writing in the fields of archaeology, mathematics and astronomy.

In the 1860s Talbot became more and more reclusive, rarely leaving the surroundings of his home. He interested himself with the running of his estates, the abbey and the village, although in 1867 he did travel to France to visit the Great Exhibition in Paris.

Ten years later, back at Lacock, Talbot died at the age of seventy-seven. The abbey passed to his son, Charles Henry Talbot, who held the estates until his death in 1916. As Charles died a bachelor, the estate passed from him to Fox Talbot's grand-daughter, Matilda, the niece of Charles Henry, who died in 1958 at the age of eighty-six. The abbey was by then owned by the National Trust, to which Matilda had presented it in 1944.

The abbey today is tenanted by members of the Burnett-Brown family, descended from Matilda Talbot's brother.

The last encounter with photography in the ageing inventor's life was in 1874 when, for the second time, he declined the presidency of the Photographic Society.

So much of Talbot's photographic work laid the foundations of modern photography that, despite the restrictions he placed upon the development of the craft and the control he tried to exercise over it, none would deny him the title of 'father of modern photography'. There is every likelihood that had Fox Talbot never worked in photography, then others would eventually have come up with the same answers as he did – and perhaps not much later. But there is no doubt that the history of photography would be much less interesting without the life story of the highly colourful and fascinating genius of William Henry Fox Talbot.

The extrovert Daguerre, who gave his invention to the French nation with a typically French gesture, did so for glory and profit. Talbot's reasons were less simple – and certainly not pure profit, as his own family often commented that he did not appear to be doing as well financially as Daguerre. Henry seems to have been spurred on by the need to do something worthwhile – and to have that something universally recognised.

A further curious twist to the story of photography is that Silvester Laroche, who by his fight had helped release photography from the licence constraints which had been placed upon its use (at a personal cost of over £500) received little help from his fellows when he asked for their support. One gift of £100 was his only thanks for an expensive fight which benefited thousands.

The salient feature of Fox Talbot's character that emerges from a study of the man is his overwhelming energy. Surely no other man in the history of the subject expended so much energy and exhibited so much involvement in such a variety of subjects as he did. His process was short-lived, but its ideals and his vision live on in the negative-positive processes of today.

PRINCIPAL EVENTS OF FOX TALBOT'S LIFE

1800   William Henry Fox Talbot born at Melbury House in Dorset.
        His father dies.
1804   His mother, Lady Elizabeth, remarried to Captain Feilding.
1808   Starts school at Rottingdean and later Harrow.
1815   Leaves Harrow and studies under private tutor for two years.
1817   Joins Trinity College, Cambridge.
1821   Graduates with Honours.
1822   Admitted to the Royal Astronomical Society.
1822-6 Joseph Nicephore Niepce produces first successful photograph
        in France.
1827   Moves to Lacock Abbey.
1828   Carries out modification to Lacock's south wing, adding the
        lattice window which would feature in his most famous
        negative.
1831   Becomes a Member of the Royal Society.
1832   Becomes a Fellow of the Royal Society. Enters politics as a
        Whig.
1832   Wins Chippenham election for a seat in the First Reform
        Parliament.
1832   Marries Constance Mundy.
1833   On honeymoon in Italy. The first ideas for the calotype process
        are formulated.
1834   Probable date for first successful experiments with Photogenic
        Drawing.
1835   Withdraws from politics.
1835   First camera negative (a Photogenic Drawing) is produced
        of the lattice window at Lacock.
1835   World's first photo-micrograph (of a crystal) produced using
        the Photogenic Drawing process and a solar microscope.
1839   The daguerreotype is announced in France.
1840   Patent No. 8650 'Obtaining Motive Power'.
1841   Patent No. 8842 'Photographic Pictures', including the basic
        specification for the calotype process.
1841   Patent No. 9167 'Coating and Colouring Metallic Surfaces'.
1842   Patent No. 9528 'Gilding and Silvering Metals'.
1843   Patent No. 9753 'Improvements in Photography', including

refinements to the calotype process designed to improve visual clarity and transparency.

1845	Patent No. 10539 'Obtaining and Applying Motive Power'.
1846	Patent No. 11475 'Obtaining and Applying Motive Power'.
1846	Patent internal combustion engine designs are announced.
1849	Patent No. 12906 'Photography' – includes procedures for printing on porcelain, and for printing on steel as a guide to engravers.
1851	Patent No. 13664 'Photography', including a modification of the albumen on glass process.
1851	Frederick Scott Archer publishes collodion process.
1852	Patent No. 565 'Engraving', an early patent for the use of bichromated gelatin on steel as an early method of photo-etching.
1852	Proposal to form a Photographic Society is published by Roger Fenton.
1853	Talbot agrees to relax patent restrictions for amateur use. Inaugural meeting of Photographic Society is held.
1854	Talbot v. Laroche. Paul Pretsch's Photo-Galvanographic process is patented.
1857	Talbot v. Pretsch.
1858	Patent No. 875 'Engraving', the patent which described Talbot's 'Photoglyphic Engraving' process using an electrotyped gutta-percha matrix.
1859	Talbot works on the cuneiform inscriptions at Nineveh.
1860	Retires to Lacock and becomes semi-recluse.
1867	Visits Great Exhibition in Paris.
1874	Declines Presidency of the Photographic Society for the second time.
1877	Fox Talbot dies at the age of seventy-seven.

The entrance archway at Lacock Abbey (opposite page) was built in 1754 by Sanderson Miller on the instructions of John Ivory Talbot, Henry Fox Talbot's great-grandfather. Through the arch can be seen William Sharrington's Tudor clock-tower, built in the early 1550s.

WHERE TO FIND OUT ABOUT FOX TALBOT

William Henry Fox Talbot is a man about whom a great number of short accounts have been written, mainly in photographic histories of a general nature.

The Fox Talbot Museum at Lacock and Lacock Abbey itself are the obvious places to find out about his life and work at first hand. Many of his possessions are there, and the house is furnished as he and his successors designed it. There are a number of photographs of him together with his certificate of Fellowship of the Royal Photographic Society and other personal effects. The house is now owned by the National Trust and is open most afternoons.

The Fox Talbot Museum, which hosts exhibitions of both historical and contemporary photography, in addition to its celebration of Talbot's life and work, is open daily.

Many of Talbot's papers and photographs were donated by Matilda Talbot to the Science Museum and are now preserved at the National Museum of Photography, Film and Television in Bradford. Talbot and his work figure strongly in the museum's permanent exhibition on the evolution of photography.

The Royal Photographic Society at The Octagon, Milsom Street, Bath, also has Talbot material.

Other museums have isolated items relevant to Talbot's life and work, and some material generally relevant to the photography of the period can usually be found in most large museums and libraries.

BIBLIOGRAPHY

Arnold, H.J.P. *William Henry Fox Talbot.* Hutchinson Benham, 1977.

Brettell, Richard R.; with Roy Flukinger, Nancy Keeler and Sydney Mallett Kilgore. *Paper and Light – The Calotype in France and Great Britain 1839-1870.* David R. Godine, 1984.

Buckland, Gail. *Fox Talbot and the Invention of Photography.* Scolar Press, 1980.

Gernsheim, Helmut. *Origins of Photography.* Thames & Hudson, 1982.

Lassam, Robert. *Fox Talbot: Photographer.* Compton Press/Dovecote Press, 1979.

Talbot, Matilda. *My Life and Lacock Abbey.* Written by the lady who donated the house to the National Trust and the pictures to the Science Museum.

Talbot, William Henry Fox. *The Pencil of Nature.* 1844-6. This book was reprinted in the USA in the 1970s and some museums and libraries will have it.

Talbot, William Henry Fox. *Sun Pictures in Scotland.* 1845. Talbot's second book and somewhat harder to find.

Thomas, D.B. *The First Negatives.* Science Museum, 1966.

Ward, John, and Stevenson, Sara. *Printed Light: The Scientific Art of William Henry Fox Talbot, and David Octavius Hill with Robert Adamson.* Scottish National Portrait Gallery, 1986.

British Journal of Photography Annual, 1966. An easier way of seeing at least part of *The Pencil of Nature,* which was reprinted in this annual.

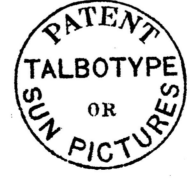

Index

Page numbers in italic refer to illustrations.